Mehndi Designs
COLORING BOOK

Marty Noble

DOVER PUBLICATIONS, INC.
MINEOLA, NEW YORK

Bibliographical Note

Mehndi Designs Coloring Book contains all the plates from the following previously published Dover books by Marty Noble: *Mehndi Designs: Traditional Henna Body Art* and *Magnificent Mehndi Designs.*

International Standard Book Number

ISBN-13: 978-0-486-80353-1
ISBN-10: 0-486-80353-8

Manufactured in the United States by RR Donnelley
80353804   2015
www.doverpublications.com